THE DEPARTMENT OF REVENUE CHILD SUPPORT ENFORCEMENT

Secrets They Don't Want You to know

Sean Gentile

authorHOUSE®

AuthorHouse™
1663 Liberty Drive
Bloomington, IN 47403
www.authorhouse.com
Phone: 1-800-839-8640

Published by AuthorHouse 12/03/2013

ISBN: 978-1-4918-3993-5 (sc)
ISBN: 978-1-4918-3994-2 (e)

Library of Congress Control Number: 2013921780

THE DEPARTMENT OF REVENUE CHILD SUPPORT ENFORCEMENT

Behind the glass door

On the other side of the glass door which threatens no soliciting, the obscure Department of Revenue Child Support Enforcement is ripe for a fearless activist to effect change. It is home to where a parent becomes a victim, betrayed by its ineffective operations conducted by standard less staffers. Irreverence abounds as it is not only condoned by upper management, it is fostered. One can only question the real reason it exists, as class action lawsuits lie dormant. Read on to learn Sean Gentile's opinion of a place that only few escape a staffer's true disdain for the innocent, seeking only what the law allows for child support cases.

NO SOLICITING

At some of the Department of Revenue Child Support Enforcement offices (DOR CSE) there are signs posted on the door that read "No soliciting." When I first began my activism work in child support there was no sign on the door at the Ft. Lauderdale Florida office. Possibly the sign is posted now to inhibit any new ideas from anyone. Your guess is as good as mine.

NO NAME IDENTIFICATION

Upon entering the nondescript DOR CSE a parent cannot distinguish the who's who of staff meandering the office. No name badge classification is required for staff. The staffer could pretend to not be acquainted with the manager, and if the staffer is the manager he could pretend otherwise to avoid his responsibilities. It is a hide and seek game to locate a staffer for assistance. It's no fun at all.

NO PICTURE OF THE MANAGER POSTED

Unlike popular grocery stores where one might feel secure shopping because of posted pictures of managers, the DOR CSE staff offers no assurance of that. There are no pictures of managers on the dirt ridden walls of the DOR CSE. The hope of help is non existent. A parent may feel something is amiss yet not fully comprehend a staffer's betrayal until it is experienced more than once. Navigating in the child support arena's endless maze of inefficiency is similar to the experience of Alice lost in Wonderland. This is not wonderland and you're not Alice.

FLAWED INFORMATION

The information a staffer emits is done haphazardly. It is given without authentic communication with the parent. A parent should not trust the staffer completely, unless the information from the staffer is in writing, analyzed and discussed with an expert like myself outside of the child support office. Scrutinize it all completely.

COMPUTER DATA NEEDS TO BE CHECKED BY ANOTHER SOURCE

Court dates that are viewed on a computer screen are not to be believed unless verified by another source. One attorney from the Office of the Attorney General (OAG) assured me that my court date was on a particular day. His computer screen revealed the court date. When I attempted to verify it at the clerks office, there was no court date as the attorney indicated. The OAG contracts with the DOR CSE for the issues of child support. Everything that is prepared by the attorneys at the OAG needs to be checked out for maximum results for a successful case result. Many times the attorneys do not read over cases prior to the court date. Therefore many attorneys are ill prepared and a poor final judgement ensues. Makes you wonder why they bother to attend the court date.

THE STAFFERS MANNERS ARE MOSTLY NONEXISTENT

It is important to know that the staffers have freedom to flamboyantly act out their ungracious ways. Parents feel ignored by the staffer's lack of salutations and dishonest case information. There is a way of tolerating their bad manners: Parents could view the staffer's behavior as a ridiculous flea market carnival show and take comfort in the humor. However, most parents yearn for effective case action so the staffers ill mannered display can be truly heartbreaking. Taking an aspirin won't even help.

MANY STAFFERS AGGRESSIVELY SHRED YOUR SELF ESTEEM AND DISSUADE YOU FROM ACTION ON YOUR CASE

"You are out for revenge!" "Whenever you get your act together." "You eat, breathe and dream child support!" This was said to me when I began the activism work! "Don't excessively call us." "We will call you." "You are so demanding." These tactics are meant to create self doubt so you passively accept the next staffer's emotional brutality. Don't accept it! Stay strong.

PUNCH IN YOUR SOCIAL SECURITY NUMBER

When a parent approaches the front desk area which is encased in impenetrable glass, the staffer immediately states without establishing polite eye contact, "Punch in your social security number." "Have a seat." Numbers called are blaring over the loud speaker beckoning victims to endure rude non information from unhappy staffers. Stick to your goals!

SECURITY GUARDS GAB WITH EACH OTHER AS PARENTS ARE IGNORED

At some DOR CSE offices the security guards sloppily sit in chairs and gab with other guards. It is as if they are perplexed that a parent has arrived at the office wanting help. Parents are ignored and the guards entertain each other with meaningless chatter.

THE WALLS REVEAL A LACK OF PRIORITIES

The child support arena involves everyone; children, mothers, fathers, attorneys, judges, legislators, activists and the public. It takes most everyone's effort to some degree to effect change and establish successful negotiations . When parents peruse sparse posters on the walls depicting only pregnant woman , the feeling is clear: According to most staff at the DOR CSE pregnant women are the only people in child support. Imagine the walls illuminating the mayor, governor, manager, fathers, mothers, children and your child support activist Sean Gentile. Wouldn't a parent feel more secure? Wouldn't it help the staffers as well to view all the people truly involved? They may finally realize that a parent has value and deserves excellent service!

THE PUBLIC SERVICE ANNOUNCEMENT SPEAKER ON THE TV MONITOR LULLS YOU WITH "SPIN"

Sometimes a DOR CSE office has a video playing depicting an attorney general claiming that the DOR CSE staff is "deeply committed" to ensuring success on your case. The only problem with that information is that it is not entirely accurate. The seeker of support is encouraged by this attorney general to be a passive recipient not a fully engaged participant. The attorney general goes on to say "It is not necessary to excessively call the DOR CSE ...it will not speed up your case." So indirectly her meaning is to be actionless. "Believe Me," she falsifies: The slow speaking attorney general is loaded with "spin". Her advise doesn't work. The DOR CSE staff is not deeply committed. Ask the thousands of parents who are disheartened from improper case action. Call often, but call the right people, with back-up.

BROCHURES ARE KEPT BEHIND THE GLASS OUT OF REACH

For some inconvenient reason plainly designed brochures that are intended to vaguely assist eager parents are hidden behind the office's misunderstood glass. A parent may be too embarrassed to ask for the brochure and the staffers don't offer.

STAFFERS SMILE TO TRICK YOU

I accompanied my client, Joe to the DOR CSE. After approval from staffers to allow me, the activist, to be able to negotiate for Joe with a staffer, Joe asked his long awaited question to the staffer: "Can I get a modification?" I was surprised when the staffer smiled and said, "Yes!" I knew this was untrue. The staffer did not qualify him whatsoever. My client needed a significant change in circumstances in order to qualify for a reduction. His income was the same. I spoke up and said, "If his income did not change and there are no other changes in circumstances then would he still qualify for a modification?" I then pointed to her to give the answer and at that moment she strongly said, "No." Joe's heart sank. The staffer initially gave a false smile and neglected to qualify him to expeditiously hustle him out of her office. If Joe had listened to her he would have wasted countless hours and dollars completing paperwork , using gas, court costs, parking, stamps, process serving and time lost from work. She had no guilt knowing that Joe would have had to endure all that waste just to stand in front of a judge approximately eight weeks later and be declined for the modification.

DIRT SMUDGES ON THE WALLS FORESHADOW FILTH SPEWED BY HURTFUL STAFFERS

Pride in an establishment shows through in the cleanliness as well as the politeness from staffers. Dirt smudges on the walls, impolite staffers evoke the true feelings of most who are employed. The rights of parents are not on the forefront of the operations at the DOR CSE. So the filth I speak of means offensive to decency. It also means a lack of propriety; lack of conforming with accepted standards of behavior. The dirt of betrayal envelopes most of the parent's experience at the DOR CSE. Carry along some disinfectant hand wipes. Document everything!

NO AUTHENTICITY FROM STAFFERS

Staffers priorities are not about authentically understanding the parents priorities of their case. When I glanced at the wall, in one of the stifling offices in which a staffer was to assist us, I noticed that her calendar for the month had eight smiley faces drawn on the weekend days. Could it be that Monday through Friday, the days to assist parents with no happy faces drawn, are truly days that there is no happiness? I think that glum greyness like a rain swelled cloud sums up most staffers attitude. I was saddened and hurt. The lack of smiley faces said it all, as well as the disinterested look on her face.

STAFFERS SPEAK ABOUT   MOST EVERYTHING AROUND YOUR CASE THAN ACTUALLY HOW TO FIX YOUR CASE

Beware how staffers tell you long winded stories about how a judge, employer or computer printout improperly created the situation with your case. Does one hour of hearing what you already know solve your problem? Request to get to the solution and don't listen to time-wasters.

SPIN TO STOP TRUE CASE SOLUTIONS

A man had an arrears payment of 30,000. For 3 years he attempted to get it corrected by requesting an audit. For three years the Department staffers repeatedly told him to "get an audit" even though he attempted to no avail.   He called me for support. I explained the situation to the staffer and instead of her being appalled at this constant error by the Department,   she ordered me: "Watch your tone." Thirty thousand dollars of error, no audit, no regret from this staffer. She then told me in front of my client "You will need to get an audit." Right then I knew it was time to stop the deceit. "He has been trying to get results from an audit for three years." I informed her. After the hemming and hawing by the staffer, with my persuasion, we had the manager notified and with the internal workings the problem was solved in one hour. My client walked out of the office only owing $900. The discrepancy that the Department faultered with was so serious that it bordered on fraud.

The precarious line drawn by the Department for my client was one of pending incarceration, license suspension and credit destruction. Yet for three years no one cared enough at the Department to help him. The staffers syrupy "spin" eclipsed any truth. When things were corrected to the true amount of $900, the joy on my clients face emanated potent relief. It is retained in my brain forever. Profound action, results in one hour. The Department of Revenue Child Support Enforcement took three years of wasted time.

MORE SPIN TO THWART PROGRESS ON CASE ACTION

When a custodial parent tries to collect child support and actually begs for help from a staffer to file for contempt, the staffer will reply: "The non-custodial parent has a pending court action for time-sharing so we will wait to see those results first before we go back to court for enforcement. The staffer is informing that no action will be taken. When a contempt hearing is actually the correct action regardless of any pending time-sharing by the other party. Yet when a non-custodial parent has a pending court action for time-shareing the staffer will tell him that it won't matter, all enforcement measures will continue. A staffer may state, "If there's a pending court action, you still need to make a payment." Granted the father/non-custodial needs to make a support payment, yet the staffer is too indifferent to thoroughly explain the process honestly to both the mother/custodial or the father/non - custodial.

THE 800 NUMBER OPERATORS DO NOT GIVE OUT ACCURATE INFORMATION MOST OF THE TIME

Be prepared to wait 30-45 minutes on the line 800 line if it is not already a straight busy signal. Asking for information on this line from an operator is usually useless. Often times after you have waited for an operator and finally do hear her voice, the operator claims to not hear your voice on the line and then terminates the call. The initial call was nothing but a frustrating experience.

THE MANAGER WILL ALWAYS BE OUT OF THE OFFICE OR IN A MEETING

For 10 years I called Tallahassee seeking the director. I was told he was always in a meeting. Apparently the PR man for the Deparment now retired, was very impressed that even though the director was always in a so called meeting he was chauffeured in a limousine. How is riding in a limo significant to any success of your Department? Thousands of people are starving to get their child support case resolved and all the PR representative embraces is a chauffeured driven director. That priority is in part what contributes to the erosion of effective management. Imagine being impressed by your boss riding in a car. Excuse me, a limousine.

SOMETIMES STAFF REFUSE TO PUT IMPORTANT STATEMENTS IN WRITING

When asked to put statements in writing many staff members just won't do it. That is an indication that what the staffer is telling you is false. It is a true test to see if any statement would be valid should it be put to the "in writing" test.

YOUR BEHAVIOR IS CRITICIZED AS THE STAFFER'S BEHAVIOR IS ABOVE REPROACH

As the staffer speaks non truths about your case it is important to watch the dynamic of how s/he speaks to you regarding your behavior. You voice tone is to be low. You are to be polite. Or else s/he will point out that you are being rude. You are to remain totally calm while you are being treated in a way that is DISHONEST, IMPOLITE and to the detriment of your well being. Funny how a staffer will value your behavior as behavior that needs to be exemplary while the staffer's behavior is standardless.

STAFFERS TELL NON TRUTHS TO MANAGER

When I was assisting my friend, Tom, a decent man who needed to collect child support from his drug addicted ex-wife, an entire year elapsed with no enforcement. The enforcement failed due to the fact that staffers ignored him when he simply asked: "Why wasn't the support being income deducted from the mother's work? " They lied continuously that papers would be coming in the mail and that Tom should wait until further notice. Nothing happened with the case. The waiting was fruitless. Meanwhile, $4,000 accrued in delinquency payments as Tom struggled to support his daughter. It was then Tom called me. Dressed with child support T-shirts illuminating "Sean Gentile is my best friend in child support," Tom and I marched into the support office. Armed with an arsenal of knowledge and a 14 year history of child support activism work, I was by his side ready for action. Our number was called and amid the stares by needy parents, we proceeded to face our staff worker. Once behind the entrance door we sat behind impenetrable glass and faced an emotional worker. "I hate activists," she claimed half joking. There was no joke. Four thousand dollars Tom's child did not receive, as well as his fruitless phone calls pleading for action and stonewalling by the very people that are supposed to help. Things changed immediately. The staffer expeditiously called the manager and complained that I threw her my card. Imagine that. How could I "throw" her my card under a tiny hand slot in the glass. We witnessed the first lie. Then as we explained the problem with the case, the worker said "Look I have only been here three months and I don't want stress.

"When she explained that, I understood that she could only handle so much. She also indicated that she used to earn so much in the business world that she took a pay cut to work at the child support office. She seemed unconcerned that Tom's case was not thoroughly enforced. Since I was there, the manager was on the phone and the real action was to commence. Another supervisor came in. The supervisor called the ex-wife's boss and reviewed the previous income deduction order that was in fact sent. This was a significant call because the ex and her boss were living together and refusing to comply with the income deduction order. What should have been done a year ago was being done for Tom's case now. The action of that phone call to the Mother's employment initiated because I was there. My 14 years of experience included 20 news articles, 3 authored books, and countless letters to the child support office in major US cities as well as legislation and frequent trips to local offices to keep a solid presence. Within two weeks Tom started receiving the money for his daughter and had a pending contempt hearing for the past year of case non-payment. The enforcement on this case was finally successfully completed despite any lie to the manager or any past discrepancies. Tom's joy oozed satisfactorily. His validation was actualized. Persistence paid off. I felt the exhilaration as well. I corrected the flaws of the Child Support Enforcement. Priceless.

WHAT IS TOLD TO YOU WILL LIKELY NOT HAPPEN

Many parents are told to accept the staffer's answer, wait for phone calls and mail regarding their case. What can usually be completed in 15 minutes at the child support office sometimes takes years simply because the staffers get away with ineffectiveness. Many times children don't get the necessities of life such as food, shelter and clothing. Imagine wanting to trust the child support office staff to find that not only in most cases you cannot trust them, you will need an education on how to penetrate the apathetic mind of the sub-standard staffer. I was fortunate enough to have strong boundaries when being violated. My anger orchestrated my course of action in my studies of the Department of Revenue's failings. My energy abounded and a passion burned inside so fierce that I would accept nothing short of excellence. I demanded it from the unenthused staffer. This cause of child support negotiations became my true love. Everything I did was for that. They knew it.

YOU ARE ALLOWED TO RECEIVE A COPY OF YOUR ENTIRE CASE

The Department staffers don't always alert you to your rights about your case history. Seems like it's cloaked in a clandestine mystery. It's not that mysterious. Just ask to see your entire case history. It is your right.

THE STAFFERS BEHAVIOR IS HAPHAZARDLY CRUEL

In the previous secrets I mentioned ill manners, lack of case action and odd behavior from staffers. I 've relentlessly analyzed how a wretched disdain for parents continues on and on. After 15 years, I've concluded: This happens in part because it is condoned by management. It is also allowed by parents who seek support for their cases. The parents give up. Another reason: Staffers behave ill mannerly because it is in part who they are. This type of human attracted to the job is one that feels comfortable in a falsely secure bureaucratic environment in which any positive change is unlikely fostered. The human spirit is usually not celebrated. Low standards are relished and most all settle for subhuman treatment. Lackluster performance ensues. Some of those very employees, though disappointed with their employment, are unsuccessful in the private sector because of a lack of energy, uncomfortability with the unknown and plain laziness. They are fearful. These psychological factors abound as non-effective operations are carried out. It is similar to any major abusive situation. Parents bang their heads against a wall to figure why the abuse is happening. There is no rhyme or reason for it. Although this is certain: Internal rage permeates every aspect of the staffers delivery of apathetic failings every day at the Department of Revenue Child Support Enforcement. It is inexcusable.

THE DEPARTMENT PERSONNEL DO NOT ENCOURAGE THE ATTORNEYS FROM THE OAG TO SEEK FULL ENFORCEMENT OF A DELINQUENT ORDER WHEN IN THE COURT ROOM

On several occasions with my own particular case, I sat on one side of the table in the magistrate's chambers, three of the Department staffers, on the other side. My ex was delinquent approximately 3 months worth of support therefore owing approximately $1,200.00. He had the ability to pay and the willful refusal to do so. He was not complying with the court ordered $400 per month. According to law the full amount could have been enforced. However, one painful reality is that the attorneys and the child support personnel inside the courtroom only request one month's worth of a purge payment. For example: Twelve hundred is owed yet the attorney only requests a $400 purge payment. This makes no logical sense. When this act is done the arrears add up astronomically. I added my knowledge and requested a full purge from the magistrate. The magistrate negated the attorney's request and agreed with me. I received the $1200 purge. This rarely happens for other parents. It is sometimes reserved for the few in the know.

THE ATTORNEYS FROM THE OAG RARELY READ ALL THE CASE INFORMATION PRIOR TO THE ACTUAL DAY OF COURT

Attorneys do not thoroughly prepare for your case. It is a mass production of semi-nonenforcement in front of the usual magistrates. Sometimes I would need to fax information to the attorney's office for them to be prepared or I directly go see them. When I do that they are clear to point out that they are "Not supposed to talk to me or any other parents." Even though that is said they still do talk to me. It is vital to know who the attorney for your case is as well as how to communicate with them. The name of the attorney is usually on the bottom right of the paperwork, along with the fax and phone number. Utilize it!

THE STAFFERS IN THE COURTROOM DO NOT SPEAK TO YOU OR ESTABLISH EYE CONTACT

When you first go to court for enforcement it feels humiliating when none of the Department staffers speak to you, or look at you. It is as if this whole process of enforcement is an embarassment. It seems it is based in shame. Are the attorneys or staffers indifferent in the courtroom so they refuse to ask for the entire amount of the delinquency purged? What harm would it be for the attorney in that courtroom to request what the law allows demand the full amount that is owed providing the payor of support has the ability to pay. Where is the justice? And where is the concern?

THE MAGISTRATE DOESN'T ALWAYS CONTROL THE COURTROOM PROPERLY

When I was in the magistrate's chamber I was speaking about my case and my ex began speaking. The magistrate had no assertiveness to stop my ex from speaking. I asked the magistrate if I could finish my bit of information. The magistrate said nothing when I asked to be able to finish speaking. So I did what the magistrate should have done: "When I am talking you are quiet." I chided my ex. I never understood why assertive acts in a courtroom seem so difficult for the magistrate to accomplish.

MANY TIMES COURTCASES GET POSTPONED IF THE OTHER PARTY DOES NOT SHOW

An unfortunate occurance after you have waited and prepared for court when the other party is a no-show, is the fact that many judges will postpone the hearing. The judge does not have to choose to postpone it. I think it wastes valuable time. It does not foster dollars to the chilldren and/or help correct any order if need be. It is a deficit to any parent to have the case postponed, unless the parent agrees to it.

A judge attempted to postpone my case several years ago and I had a fervent reaction: I heard the judge tell a balif: "I will reschedule this." I was more the rebel at that time and beautifully aggressive. I was sitting in the waiting area and began talking aloud hoping the judge would hear my articulate expressions. With my press articles in hand, I loudly instructed the judge from the distant waiting area: "I know how this system works. I have been in the press over 20 times regarding my child support activism work. If this case gets postponed I will let everybody know exactly what happend. I expect my case to be heard. My voice reverberated through what felt like every single room in the courthouse. I didn't matter to me because I felt my child support activism was all that mattered and in my mind I really had nothing without this fight. So if the case was not heard that day my well being was irrelevant. I was wiling to face any consequence. I thought my case would be heard and my presence honored. That is precisely what occured. My relentless pursuit to create positive action for my case was satiated. No matter how tough I had to be. The judge did order a purge payment for the support owed and that is exactly what should have occured. The fight was worth it!

OFTEN JUDGES REFUSE TO LET YOU SPEAK ABOUT YOUR CASE

One element of frustration is a great yearning to finally tell the judge your side of the story and you start to talk when it appears to be your turn and the judge complains you are interrupting. It doesn't seem normal that a judge would tell you, you are interrupting when the courtroom was quiet. Many times in the long awaited court date you may not get the chance to express yourself. There is however something you should know: A judicial code of conduct indicates a judge should hear what you have to say if you have legal interest in the case. That is the generic idea of what should happen. In my opinion a game is played. The game is that all involved act like the knowledge they have is an unattainable mystery and you must suffer because you will never have this knowledge. I feel sadness and anger writing about the tribulations which occur. The magistrate, judges, Department staffers, attorneys all know what goes on. They all seem to pretend that what is going on is in fact the way that it should be in those magistrate's chambers. However it is not .

SOMETIMES COURT DATE NOTICES ARE MAILED AFTER THE COURT DATE

It is important to check on your court date with different sources because you cannot always rely on the court staff to mail in a timely fashion.
Some sources to check would be the judges secretary, the court web site, a court clerk and the Department of Revenue staffer. If you try all four sources you should access your court date. Do not rely on one source. Many a client has informed me that the custodial parent was mailed the court date yet the non custodial was not.

WHEN SUBMITTING PAPERWORK AT COURT OR DEPARTMENT OF REVENUE BEWARE OF IMPROPER INFORMATION AND ABUSIVE TREATMENT

The clerks at some courthouses intentionally slow down court dates due to their lack of desire to do thorough case checks. For example:When seeking a notice of hearing, with the proper "notice of hearing" paperwork in hand, some clerks ask a parent to resubmit the initial petition which was submitted the prior month. How much sense does it make to resubmit the original petition when it is already on file at the court?

They also don't assist parents if a slight error is made in the case number. Instead of pointing out the error in detail they may state a generality

such as "I can't submit this ." As If it is a mystery . Whereas a simple,"You are missing a zero in the case number."It all stems down to psychological abuse. Very easily if one is a sound thinker you can solve a problem without the antics.

ABUSIVE TREATMENT EXISTS AT THE COURTHOUSE BECAUSE THE CLERK OF COURT AT SOME LEVEL ALLOWS IT.

I can acknowledge this first hand. I have met with a clerk of court, wrote letters to the clerk of court and had an attorney write a letter to a clerk of court threatening a law suit if certain employees did not show proper respect in carrying out their tasks. Frankly he seemed indifferent to effect change.

BE ALERT TO THE FACT THAT MANY DEPARTMENT STAFFERS AND COURT STAFF MAY STATE "THE MAGISTRATE IS WELL RESPECTED" WHEN IN FACT IT MAY NOT TRUE

Just because an attorney,staffer, judge or court staff make a blatant statement regarding someone's reputation good or bad, it means nothing unless checked out. Sometimes this is told to you to control your reactions.

MANY STAFFERS OR ATTORNEYS AND COURT STAFF ADVISE "DON'T ANGER THE JUDGE" OR " STAY QUIET IN FRONT OF JUDGE"

I can never figure out why if you are "right" according to what the law dictates should you remain in a cowaring state in front of a judge. I believe it is not necessary. When any staff member advises this beware because it borders on manipulative tactics. You have rights according to the judicial code of conduct.

THE DEPARTMENT STAFFERS AND OFFICE OF THE ATTORNEY GENERAL ATTORNEY'S DO NOT REQUEST ALL THE LAW ALLOWS FROM THE JUDGE.

The attorney's should know the laws that are there to have enforced when in the courtroom; however many times they barely utter any words at all, as if to not rock any boat in front of any judge. Poor performance. Why go to law school if you dont want to have courage?

SOME JUDGES SECRETARYS RECEIVE YOUR REQUEST FOR A NOTICE OF HEARING AND STILL DO NOTHING WITH IT

I had to chase down exactly where my request for a notice of hearing went. The clerks told me to check with the judge's secretary and when I did (after walking up eight flights of stairs), the judge's secretary looked at me and said, "I saw this come across my desk already , I swore could have sent it out." She told me to wait for the mail and "If it doesn't come by Friday call me back." The notice of Hearing didn't come by Friday. I walked back up eight flights of stairs (elevators too claustrophobic for me) She repeated she was sorry and that she was new. She then saw me turn my head to her 2003 achievment on the wall. She sheepishly smiled then she said she was employed in another department. So she really wasn't new. She never mailed me the court date as she is compensated to do. Are these the type of people who we have at our courthouse? Maybe they are there just to collect a paycheck and actually enjoy all the non-effectiveness as well as the preoccupation with vacation time. I overheard her speaking to another secretary on the phone and she mentioned what days she would be on vacation. Suppose that's the priority. Work can be a vacation if you like what you do! Meanwhile the court dates are haphazardly sent out.

THE ATTORNEYS AT THE OAG RARELY REVIEW MATERIAL FOR YOUR CASE BEFORE COURT

Regarding a collection there is little preparation by the attorneys which could help you possibly receive more of a purge payment for dollars for your child. It could also effect any way the judge receives information on the status of the employment of the paying parent. Any bit of information could be vital. But rarely is it intensely studied by the attorneys at the OAG.

THE JUDGES OR MAGISTRATES PRETEND IN THE COURT HEARING THAT "YOU ARE ALWAYS INTERRUPTING" EVEN WHEN THERE IS NOT A SOUND IN THE COURTROOM

I find this point very absurd. Magistrates and judges work hard in most cases to put you on the defensive. Even if there is not one sound in the courtroom, many magistrates or judges, continually tell parents that they are interrupting when in fact there was not a sound to be heard. You must use an immense amount of internal control to handle the lack of reality in the judges chambers. It is maddening.

"TALLAHASSEE IS THE OFFICIAL RECORD KEEPER"

"How do you know Tallahassee is the official record keeper?"
Statements are randomly made that need to be clarified. However as soon as the staffer is asked to clarify what was said by her, she often denies saying it. "I didn't say that." Yes you did!

MANY TIMES STAFFERS GET LOST IN PHONY SMALL TALK

One staffer continually tried to trick a parent by asking him for several minutes who he had in the office with him. His case situation of three arrearage mistakes for one case was ignored and the most important topic was who he brought with him. "Is that your girlfriend?" "Is that the child's mother?" "Who is that?" Really unnecessary and a true show of ignorance. Solve the case.

THERE ARE MANY MISREPRESENTATIONS ONE FOR THE PARENT AND SOME FOR THE COURT

A parent filed her own motion in the court even though she had engaged the Department of Revenue Child Support Enforcement. The DOR CSE then sent her a letter stating :"Its legal provider is not authorized to pursue this motion because the parent filed it." However the DOR CSE filed a motion to the court indicated otherwise. It indicated: The parent no longer needs our services. These statements to the parent and motion to the court by the DOR CSE were completely untrue. I know this because the parent did not ask for the DOR CSE'S services to be terminated and I also have filed motions on my own in which the Department of Revenue's service provider the OAG was in fact authorized to come to court for the motion of contempt that I filed. Maybe it moved forward for me because I insist on it. Maybe because I have made a name for myself. The other parent should have been treated with the same regard for a court action as well. The director in Tallahassee was notified of this and there was no explanation by her in any return letter as I expeditiously requested. What is new?

AUTHOR BIO

Sean Gentile MBA

Sean Gentile has scrutinized the way the staffers at the Department of Revenue Child Support Enforcement and the Circuit Courts carry out the day to day operations for over 15 years. She has seen first hand the betrayal, lack of cooperation and apathy from the staffers to parents who simply seek either support or corrections on faulty support orders.

Sean Gentile has earned an MBA and has been assisting parents in all areas of child support to include family mediation. By her unique assertive style and wisdom, she reveals ways to understand that any "spin" or non action on a case should NOT inhibit any parent from persevering for effective case action.

Sean Gentile is extremely generous with her child support knowledge and assures all parents that they have value and are to be treated decently. This underlying mission gives hope and joy to thousands. Her strength and compassion allow others to have a chance to finally feel proud of their own child support accomplishments. A priceless endeavor.

No one has more enthusiasm for successful negotiations or a life long mission to elicit positive change in the child support arena.

Sean Gentile has also authored: 100 Effective Ways to Collect Child Support and 100 Effective Ways to Be an Extraordinary Parent.

Sean Gentile's earlier work has been documented in approximately 20 news articles highlighting her tenacity and determination for improvement in the child support systems.

She has parented four assertive, creative children as a single mom for the past 18 years. In the South Florida area she is well known in the child support circles. Several bench ads and media with her name inform all of her mission.

Her new child support comic book action hero, a.k.a, Sean Gentile, will continue to educate and entertain in ways to teach parents that there are many alternative solutions for child support and self development. Hence, a true collectors item. Stay tuned for more Sean Gentile.

www.facebook.com/pages/SeanGentileChildSupport
www.SeanGentileChildSupport

BANKRUPTCY
FORECLOSURE DEFENSE
Credit Restoration
Real Estate
Civil & Business Litigation

Elias Leonard Dsouza Esq.
Attorney at Law

111 N. Pine Island Rd
Suite # 205
Plantation, Fl 33324

Telephone: (954) 358-5911

Web: www.DsouzaLegal.com   E-mail: dtdlaw@aol.com
FREE INITIAL CONSULTATION • PAYMENT PLANS AVAILABLE

➔ **FOCUS OF PRACTICE:** Bankruptcy Law, Foreclosure Defense, Defence of Credit Card Lawsuits & Credit Restoration

➔ **BAR MEMBERSHIP:** Florida Bar (2000) United States District Court, Southern Northern & Middle District of Florida

➔ **LEGAL PRACTICE:** Shareholder - Law office of Elias Leonard Dsouza, P.A. Since 2000 represented over 1500 individuals

➔ **MISSION:** Very Passionate about Consumer Protect their Rights. Assist people to "get a fresh financial start".

21

NOTES

NOTES

NOTES

NOTES

NOTES

NOTES

NOTES

NOTES

NOTES

NOTES

NOTES

NOTES

NOTES

NOTES

NOTES

NOTES

NOTES

NOTES

NOTES

NOTES

NOTES

Printed in the United States
By Bookmasters